Phillis Wheatley

PHILLIS WHEATLEY, NEGRO SERVANT to Mr. JOHN WHEATLEY, of BOSTON.

JUNIOR ■ WORLD ■ BIOGRAPHIES

Phillis Wheatley

VICTORIA SHERROW

CHELSEA JUNIORS

a division of CHELSEA HOUSE PUBLISHERS

Chelsea House Publishers
EDITOR-IN-CHIEF: Remmel Nunn
MANAGING EDITOR: Karyn Gullen Browne
COPY CHIEF: Mark Rifkin
PICTURE EDITOR: Adrian G. Allen
ART DIRECTOR: Maria Epes
ASSISTANT ART DIRECTOR: Howard Brotman
MANUFACTURING DIRECTOR: Gerald Levine
SYSTEMS MANAGER: Lindsey Ottman
PRODUCTION MANAGER: Joseph Romano
PRODUCTION COORDINATOR: Marie Claire Cebrián

JUNIOR WORLD BIOGRAPHIES

SENIOR EDITOR: Kathy Kuhtz

Staff for PHILLIS WHEATLEY
EDITORIAL ASSISTANT: Karen Akins
PICTURE RESEARCHER: Michèle Brisson
SENIOR DESIGNER: Marjorie Zaum

First Printing

1 3 5 7 9 8 6 4 2

Library of Congress Cataloging-in-Publication Data
Sherrow, Victoria.
  Phillis Wheatley/Victoria Sherrow.
     p. cm.—(Junior world biographies)
  Summary: The life of the woman who, although a slave, gained renown
throughout the colonies as the first important black American poet.
     ISBN 0-7910-1753-2
     1. Wheatley, Phillis, ca. 1754–84—Biography—Juvenile literature.
  2. Poets, American—18th century—Biography—Juvenile literature.
  3. Slaves—United States—Biography—Juvenile literature. [1. Wheatley,
Phillis, ca. 1754–84. 2. Poets, American. 3. Slaves. 4. Afro-Americans—
Biography.] I. Title. II. Series.
  PS866.W5Z695 1992   91-12767
  811'.1—dc20   CIP
  [B]   AC

Contents

The action at this Richmond, Virginia, slave auction was probably very similar to that at the auction in Boston, Massachusetts, where Susannah Wheatley purchased Phillis in 1761.

1

A Remarkable Child from Africa

In 1985, the governor of Massachusetts declared February 1 to be Phillis Wheatley Day, in honor of the Boston woman who is called the mother of black literature in America. Phillis Wheatley was a much-admired poet who lived during the late 18th century. In *colonial America*, few women, and even fewer black people, wrote poems, stories, or novels for publication. Yet

Wheatley's poems appeared in books and newspapers in America and England. She was the new nation's first well-known black author, and she was the second woman to have a book published. (Anne Bradstreet, the British-born New England poet, was the first.)

When Phillis Wheatley came to America in 1761, few people would have guessed that she would become a famous writer. Just eight years old, Phillis arrived in Boston Harbor in the hold of a cargo ship. She was 1 of 75 people who had been kept inside the ship for several months while it crossed the Atlantic Ocean. These people had been kidnapped from their homelands in Africa to be sold in America as slaves.

The journey was a harsh one. The captives spent almost every hour crowded inside the dark and dirty hold. Often they were given only rice and water to eat. It is easy to understand why young Phillis was in poor health when she finally reached Boston.

Phillis did not write much about the slave

ship or about her early life in Africa. But her first biographers thought that she was born in 1753 or 1754. Phillis probably came from Senegambia, because the other people aboard the slave ship *Phillis* were taken from that area. Today this part of western Africa is made up of two countries, Senegal and Gambia.

Phillis probably felt frightened and confused when she arrived in Boston. Still a child, she had been torn away from her home, her family, and her friends. Now she was in a strange land. She found herself standing on a wharf with other Africans while light-skinned strangers stared at her. Phillis had no clothing to wear. Somehow she found a piece of worn carpet to wrap around herself.

In 1761, there were about 230,000 blacks in colonial America. Nearly all of them were slaves, bought and "owned" by other people. Most slaves lived in the southern colonies, where they did heavy labor on large cotton, rice, and tobacco *plantations*. About 16,000 blacks lived in New England, where some slaves worked as farmhands but most worked as household servants.

A wealthy woman named Susannah Wheatley had come to the wharf that day to find a

King Street, where the Wheatleys' home was located, was often bustling with merchants, sailors, fishermen, and shopkeepers. Phillis was probably amazed by all the new sights she encountered in Boston.

personal servant. She had planned to buy an older girl. But apparently she changed her mind when she saw Phillis.

Seated in Susannah Wheatley's horse-drawn carriage, Phillis rode to her new home.

Eighteenth-century Boston probably looked odd to a child from an African village. This port city was home to fishermen, sailors in uniform, merchants, shopkeepers, and other citizens. Most people were light skinned and spoke languages Phillis had not heard in Africa. The men wore white-powdered wigs and were dressed in waistcoats, breeches, and buckled shoes. The women wore bonnets, stockings, and long skirts that rustled as they walked.

Boston Harbor smelled of fish as well as of the coffee, spices, and bananas brought by ship from other lands. Inside the bustling city were houses and stores made of wood and brick. Some buildings stood two or three stories tall. On the streets, people sold goods from stalls and pushcarts. They rang bells and called out the names of the various items they hoped to sell: oysters, chowder, oranges.

The Wheatley home was large and comfortable. It was located in a busy section of Boston that was at that time called King Street. Besides a new house in a new land, Phillis also got a new name. Her first name came from the ship on which she had sailed. Her last name became Wheatley, that of her new family.

From her first weeks with the Wheatleys, Phillis showed that she was unusually intelligent. She quickly began to master her new language, English. As she gained skill in speaking it, she worked to understand written letters and words. A woman who knew the Wheatley family later wrote that Phillis often made "letters upon the wall with a piece of chalk or charcoal."

During the 18th century, many people would have stopped Phillis from studying. For one thing, girls were not expected to be well educated. They were reared to carry out their future roles as wives and mothers. Not only was Phillis a girl; she was black. Many people wrongly thought that blacks could not learn as well as whites could. Other people feared that if blacks were educated, they would be even less willing to accept their unequal position in a society in which they were

Phillis used a goose-feather quill, like the ones shown here, to write her poems. The tips of the quills were sharpened with small blades known as penknives.

owned and controlled by whites. In southern towns, it was against the law to teach a black person how to read or write.

For reasons such as these, most white families insisted that black servants keep busy with cooking, sewing, and performing other household chores. They would have discouraged—or even forbidden—Phillis's efforts to learn from books.

Yet the Wheatleys encouraged Phillis to study. They let their 18-year-old daughter, Mary, help her gain knowledge. Together, Phillis and Mary read the Bible and other books. By the age of nine, Phillis could understand and explain difficult sections of the Bible. She also enjoyed reading poetry and reciting poems she had memorized.

At age 12, Phillis started writing her own poems. The Wheatleys gave her the tools that she needed: paper, ink, and a *quill* (a feather, plucked from a goose, that people then sharpened with the blade of a penknife). Phillis often wrote at night, so the family made certain that she had candles in her room to provide enough light for her work.

Phillis continued to suffer from poor health and frequent illnesses. She had trouble breathing, as well as a persistent cough that may have been caused by *tuberculosis* (a lung disease that had no cure at that time) or *asthma* (a lung disease that is often caused by allergies and is characterized by coughing and difficulty in breathing). Susannah Wheatley paid special attention to Phillis's health, just as she did to the girl's education. When Phillis was ill, Susannah Wheatley made sure that she had nourishing food and plenty of rest. Phillis was allowed to take relaxing visits to the countryside and accompany the Wheatleys on family vacations.

The Wheatleys often spent their vacations in Newport, Rhode Island. Like many other wealthy New Englanders, they enjoyed the pleasant summer climate and scenery of the seaside town. During these trips to Newport, Phillis spent time with Obour Tanner, who was also a slave and was the same age as Phillis. The two girls became friends.

Her friendship with Obour must have meant a great deal to Phillis. Her life with the Wheatleys had given her many privileges, including an education and a lighter work load than that of most slaves. But this special treatment set Phillis apart from other black people. She was regarded as "better" than the other slaves in the household and was not allowed to spend much time with them. Even so, Phillis remained a slave. She did not enjoy the same freedom as the white people around her did. She was treated as superior to other blacks but still had no clear place in the larger, white world.

Because she had no close black friends in Boston, Phillis found other activities to fascinate her. Literature and religion became her major interests. Her religious roots in Africa were probably in the Muslim faith. (Muslims are people who follow the monotheistic, or one God, religion of Islam, which is based on the teachings of the 7th-century prophet Muhammad.) In America, she became familiar with the religious ideas of the white people around her. Boston had been founded by English *Puritans*, members of a strict Protestant church. The Puritans had separated from the Church of England in order to start a new community in Massachusetts.

The Wheatleys worshiped at Boston's Old South Meeting House. During the late 18th century, preachers traveled throughout the colonies giving powerful sermons. They hoped that these special meetings would renew the colonists' interest in religion. Blacks were allowed to attend New England churches but had to sit apart from whites in their own rows of seats. Phillis attended Sunday services. She heard some of the sermons given by traveling ministers, such as the famous Englishman George Whitefield. She became an enthusiastic follower of the Puritan faith.

Phillis often wrote about her religious ideas in letters to friends and in her poems. When

Seventeen-year-old Phillis Wheatley was baptized in the Old South Meeting House, which still stands, in Boston. She attended Sunday services but had to sit with other blacks apart from whites in a separate section of the church.

she was 14 years old, she wrote a long poem urging people to believe in God. She said that faith in God is a vital part of life. Phillis also wrote that people should "turn . . . from the dangerous road," that is, they should resist the temptation to do evil rather than good. She believed that human beings must guard against attempts by the devil to make them commit wrongful acts, or sins.

At age 17, Phillis was baptized at the Old South Meeting House and became an official church member. She was now a young woman. Apparently, the Wheatleys were very proud of Phillis's achievements. They planned a number of social occasions so that ministers, public officials, and other important citizens could meet the remarkable African teenager in their household.

Some of them invited Phillis to their homes, too. One afternoon, Phillis found herself in the mansion of Timothy Fitch, owner of the *Phillis*. It was probably strangely awkward for Phillis to sip tea in the drawing room along with Fitch's wife and daughters.

Phillis received attention and praise for both her conversational skills and her poems. People were amazed by her fine writing, elegant manners, and intelligence. Perhaps some of them had not thought much about the plight of black people in the colonies. Or they may have shared the prejudices of the day and supposed that blacks were not as capable as whites. (A *prejudice* is a judgment or opinion, usually negative, that has been formed about something or someone before all the facts are known.) Phillis showed that this opinion was not true. Her talents and accomplishments helped others understand that black people had the same abilities as whites.

As a black woman and a slave, Phillis had overcome huge obstacles to achieve her early success. The years ahead were to be busy ones, both happy and sad. Soon the American colonies would fight a war to win their independence from England. Phillis Wheatley would be a published author on two continents. She would even be honored as the guest of a future president of the United States.

The only 18th-century likeness of Phillis Wheatley that still survives today is this engraving, which appeared in her first and only book, Poems on Various Subjects, Religious and Moral, *published in London on September 1, 1773.*

PHILLIS WHEATLEY, NEGRO SERVANT to Mr. JOHN WHEATLEY, of BOSTON.

Publifhed according to Act of Parliament, Sept.ᵗ 1, 1773 by Archᵈ. Bell.
Bookfeller Nᵒ. 8 near the Saracens Head Aldgate.

P O E M S

ON

VARIOUS SUBJECTS,

RELIGIOUS AND MORAL.

BY

PHILLIS WHEATLEY,

NEGRO SERVANT to Mr. JOHN WHEATLEY,
of BOSTON, in NEW ENGLAND.

L O N D O N:
Printed for A. BELL, Bookfeller, Aldgate; and fold by
Meffrs. COX and BERRY, King-Street, BOSTON.

M DCC LXXIII.

2

Becoming
an Author

While Phillis Wheatley was growing up during the 1760s, great changes were taking place in the American colonies. Disagreements arose between the colonies and Great Britain. In England, the *Parliament* (the British law-making body) kept raising colonial taxes. Other British laws required colonial ships to pay special fees. They said the colonists must buy only British-made goods.

Many colonists resented these laws. They did not want to give their wages to Great Britain. The colonists also did not wish to obey laws made by a king who lived thousands of miles away from them. Boston was a major port city with political leaders among its citizens. As a result, the Wheatley family witnessed exciting events. Phillis wrote poems about historical incidents that took place before and during the American War of Independence.

One such dramatic scene occurred in August 1765. Shouting "Liberty! Property! No stamps!" a group of *patriots* (those colonists who wanted freedom from British rule) paraded down Boston's streets. They spoke out against an unpopular new law called the *Stamp Act*. The Stamp Act required the colonists to buy specially marked ("stamped") paper for legal documents, such as wills and marriage certificates. They also had to use the stamped paper for newspapers, calendars, and other printed items.

The patriots who marched in Boston that August day called themselves Sons of Liberty. Other Sons of Liberty groups had formed in different towns throughout the colonies. They made speeches and gave people *pamphlets* that complained about the Stamp Act and other British laws.

Phillis may have watched and heard the Sons of Liberty. The Wheatley mansion on King Street was located along the route taken by the marchers. The Customs House, where the British collected taxes and payment for stamps from the colonists, was also located near the Wheatleys' home.

To gain more control of the region, the British government sent military troops to Boston in 1768. The colonists nicknamed the soldiers "redcoats" because of the color of their fancy uniforms. The newly arrived redcoats marched through Boston to the rhythm of beating drums. After seeing them, Phillis wrote a poem called "On the Arrival of the Ships of War, and Landing of the Troops." Unfortunately, no copy of the poem can be found today.

In 1770, a sad event led Phillis to write another poem. Some Bostonians had been arguing about whether England had the right to rule the colonies. Christopher Snider, who was 11 years old, died after being shot by Ebenezer Richardson.

In 1765, Bostonians protest the passing of the Stamp Act. The British law called for taxes on almost everything printed in the colonies to help pay for the cost of protecting and securing them by British troops.

Richardson was a *Tory* (a person loyal to the British). Phillis heard about the shooting and wrote "On the death of Mr. Snider Murder'd by

Richardson." The poem calls Christopher Snider "the first martyr for the cause." These words show that Phillis supported the patriots. The "cause" that she wrote about was that of independence.

A violent fight later known as the *Boston Massacre* took place about a month afterward, on March 5, 1770. A group of Bostonians began throwing snowballs at a British guard stationed at the Customs House. One redcoat started shooting. Three men, including a middle-aged black named Crispus Attucks, were shot by British soldiers.

Thousands of Boston citizens attended funeral services for the dead men. Phillis expressed her feelings in a poem, "On the Affray in King Street, on the Evening of the 5th of March, 1770." Again, the original manuscript and all copies of the poem have been lost. Only the title is known today.

Besides writing new poems, Phillis continued to study and learn. She read books about geography, history, and astronomy. She also studied Latin, literature, and mythology.

Phillis's interest in religion continued to grow. It was in August 1770 that she was delighted by the sermons of the English preacher George Whitefield. Whitefield said that people of all colors were equal in God's eyes. He urged everyone to love all peoples, whatever their race or social position. Although Whitefield did not work to end slavery, he suggested that it was wrong for one race of people to make slaves of another. All people have immortal souls, said Whitefield.

Phillis was sad when Whitefield died in late 1770 at the age of 56. She decided to write a poem in his honor. Like other poems written in colonial days, this one had a long and detailed title: "An Elegiac Poem on the Death of the celebrated Divine, and eminent Servant of Jesus Christ, the late Reverend, and pious George Whitefield, Chaplain to Right Honourable the Countess of Huntingdon, &c, &c, Who made his exit from this transitory State, to dwell in the Celestial Realms of Bliss, on Lord's Day, 30th of September, 1770."

The poem was printed in the form of pamphlets, which were made available to people in Philadelphia, New York, and Newport as well as

On March 5, 1770, a group of angry Bostonians heckled a redcoat standing guard at the Customs House. Pushed beyond their limit of endurance, a group of British soldiers opened fire on the civilians and killed three men in what later became known as the Boston Massacre.

Boston. In it, Phillis praised Whitefield and mourned that "we hear no more the music of thy tongue."

The poem was very popular. Soon more people knew about Phillis's talents. The pamphlet told readers that the poem had been written "by

Phillis, a Servant Girl of 17 Years of Age, belonging to Mr. J. Wheatley, of Boston:—and has been but 9 years in this Country from Africa." Many people who read and liked the poem may have been surprised that the author was not only so young but also a slave.

The poem was sent to Whitefield's friends and followers in Great Britain. The British readers liked the poem, too. Phillis Wheatley became famous on two continents.

By 1772, Susannah Wheatley firmly believed that a collection of Phillis's poems should be published as a book. But first she had to convince a printer that he would earn enough money by publishing the volume. In those days, printers expected authors to make a list of people who would buy the finished book. Printers asked Susannah Wheatley to find at least 300 people who would promise to buy Phillis's book of poetry.

Susannah Wheatley put advertisements in a Boston newspaper. She wrote the names of 28 poems that would be in the book and asked people to sponsor it. But not enough people agreed to sign the list. Susannah Wheatley tried for several months, but she could not get enough names to convince a printer to publish the volume.

While Susannah Wheatley worked to get the poetry book published, Phillis kept writing. She sent an unusual and powerful poem to William Legge, who had just been named the secretary of state in North America. Legge had opposed the Stamp Act and was a follower of George Whitefield's. Phillis thought that perhaps Legge would share her feelings about slavery and freedom. In the poem, Phillis tells how she was kidnapped in Africa, then sold as a slave. She asks, "What sorrows labour in my parent's breast?" as a result of losing their child to slavery. After describing her feelings, she writes:

Such, such my case. And can I then but pray-
Others may never feel tyrannic sway?

The poem was unusual because it expressed personal feelings. In the 18th century, poets were expected to describe events in graceful words, without emotion. But in this poem, Phillis voices her desire for freedom. She says that humans should not be kept as slaves.

At about this time, Susannah Wheatley gave up hope of getting Phillis's book published in Boston. She decided to look for a London printer instead. Susannah Wheatley went to Captain Robert Calef, who worked on a ship owned by the Wheatleys. She asked him to show the poems to printers in London during his next voyage there.

In London, Captain Calef met a small religious printer, Archibald Bell. Bell read Phillis's poetry and agreed to publish it. But Bell told Calef that he must bring him proof that Phillis Wheatley was really a black slave.

Back in Boston, Susannah Wheatley collected the signatures of 18 important Boston citizens. They all confirmed that Phillis Wheatley

The British preacher George Whitefield inspired Phillis with his sermons about racial equality. When Whitefield died, she wrote an elegy, or mournful poem, to honor him.

was a black slave. Later, the same list of names was printed inside Phillis's book.

Then Susannah Wheatley made up a package containing the list of names, 39 of Phillis's poems, and 2 sections called *prefaces* that would be printed at the beginning of the book. Phillis wrote one preface, and John Wheatley the other. The prefaces spoke of the problems Phillis had overcome when she successfully learned to speak and write in a strange new language, English.

Phillis still had another important decision to make: She needed to decide to whom she should dedicate her book. In those days, a book usually sold more copies if it was dedicated to an important person. Susannah Wheatley thought that the countess of Huntingdon was an excellent choice. The countess had strongly supported the preacher George Whitefield, and she admired the poem that Phillis had written in Whitefield's honor.

Printer Archibald Bell arranged a meeting with the countess. He read Phillis's poems to her during his visit. Early in 1773, the countess of Huntingdon agreed that Phillis could dedicate the book to her. She also suggested that a portrait of Phillis be printed inside the book.

The picture that appeared in the volume shows Phillis Wheatley as a slim young woman with large dark eyes. She sits thoughtfully at a desk, writing with a quill pen. The young poet wears a simple dress and a white ruffled cap. This likeness is the only one of Phillis Wheatley that exists today.

No one is sure who painted the portrait that was used to make engraved pictures of Phillis for the book. But some historians think the artist was a black slave named Scipio Moorhead. The Moorheads were friends of the Wheatleys'. Besides, Phillis must have known Moorhead. Her book includes a poem called "To S.M., a Young African Painter."

People in London began to hear about Phillis Wheatley's poetry and the book that Archibald Bell was going to publish. Like people in the colonies, many Londoners were amazed that such remarkable poetry had been written by a person who was not only young and female but also a black slave.

Phillis Wheatley became a book author at the age of 20. Her fame grew in England. But her health, never good, worsened. Susannah Wheatley's doctor said that an ocean voyage might improve Phillis's physical condition.

Hearing this suggestion, Susannah Wheatley thought that a voyage to London would be good for Phillis's health. It would also advance her career as a poet. The Wheatleys' son, Nathaniel, planned to sail to England in the spring of 1773. Susannah Wheatley decided that Phillis should travel with him. She wrote to the countess of Huntingdon, telling her that the young poet would arrive in England in June. The countess knew many important people, including writers and artists. The countess of Huntingdon told them about Phillis's planned visit.

Susannah Wheatley also informed newspapers in New York and other cities that Phillis Wheatley would soon visit England, where her book was to be published. Then she sent a copy of Phillis's new poem, "A Farewell to America," to the editor of a London newspaper. With the poem, Susannah Wheatley sent a letter. It said that Phillis had achieved success as a poet because of natural talent and "through her own application [effort], unassisted by others."

In 1761, eight-year-old Phillis was homeless and alone as she crossed the ocean in a crowded slave ship. When 19-year-old Phillis Wheatley sailed for England on May 8, 1773, she was known to newspaper readers as an "extraordinary Negro poet." She looked forward to meeting the important people who awaited her in England. But what probably thrilled her even more about the trip was the thought of actually witnessing the publication of her book, *Poems on Various Subjects, Religious and Moral.*

Benjamin Franklin, the American statesman, scientist, and philosopher, met Phillis Wheatley while she was visiting London in the spring of 1773.

CHAPTER

3

Fame and
Freedom

Phillis probably expected that people in London would be kind to her. Even so, she was surprised at the wonderful welcome she received there. After her trip, Phillis wrote to her friend Obour Tanner that she had made many friends "among the nobility and the gentry," people with royal titles and great wealth.

Friends of the countess of Huntingdon's had planned parties and teas so that Londoners could meet the celebrated young poet. The famous American writer, statesman, and scientist Benjamin Franklin was in London, too. Phillis met him during her visit.

But the most thrilling event for Phillis was meeting the lord mayor of London. He gave her an old copy of the well-known poem *Paradise Lost*. Written during the 1660s by the English poet John Milton, the poem is considered by most scholars to be the greatest epic written in the English language. It is the story of Satan's rebellion against God and the banishment of Adam and Eve from the Garden of Eden. Phillis had admired Milton's work for several years, and she cherished the valuable copy of *Paradise Lost*.

Phillis had great plans for the rest of her stay in England. The countess of Huntingdon had asked her to visit her grand house in Wales. And Phillis was thrilled that she would be in England when her book was finally printed. Her early biographers also believe that her London admirers hoped that she would be invited to meet King George III when he returned to his London palace that autumn.

Unfortunately, Phillis had to leave England less than a month after she arrived. Susannah Wheatley sent a message to London saying that she was very ill. She told Phillis to return home. Phillis boarded the ship *London* and headed back to Boston.

Meanwhile, the first copies of Phillis's book of poetry were printed in England. Archibald Bell had placed several ads in the newspapers to announce the publication of the book. He praised the poetry as "one of the greatest instances of pure, unassisted genius, that the world ever produced."

Newspaper reviews of Phillis's book *Poems on Various Subjects, Religious and Moral* praised her writing. But reviewers also used the opportunity to speak out against the white colonists who made Phillis a slave. They criticized

Americans who talked about their love of freedom while keeping people such as Phillis in slavery.

Shortly after Phillis returned to America, the Wheatley family set her free. She was no longer a slave, but she stayed in the Wheatley home. Susannah Wheatley was very sick. Phillis spent much time caring for the bedridden woman.

During the first months of 1774, Phillis waited eagerly for copies of her books to arrive from London. Now that she was free, she had to support herself with her own money. She began looking for people who would buy her books after they arrived. Phillis asked friends, including Obour Tanner, to help her find buyers for the newly published poems.

As a free woman, Phillis Wheatley began to speak out more strongly against slavery. In February 1774, she wrote a letter to Sampson Occom, a Mohegan Indian who had become a Christian minister. Phillis wrote that God had given every human being "love of freedom." She said that it did not make sense when people

This 18th-century printing press, which was designed by Benjamin Franklin, is very much like the one used to print Phillis Wheatley's poems.

owned other human beings and then claimed to be true Christians. It was greed, declared Phillis, that led slave owners to ignore the suffering of blacks.

These words were very strong, coming from a black woman in colonial days. Occom must have shared the letter with other people, because it was printed in the *Connecticut Gazette* in March 1774. Other editors noticed the letter and decided to reprint it in their newspapers.

Just before her words were printed and discussed, Phillis suffered a great personal loss. Susannah Wheatley died on March 3, 1774, at the age of 65. Phillis wrote a sorrowful letter to Obour Tanner, saying that she felt that she had lost a family member. She wrote, "I was a poor little outcast and stranger when she took me in; not only into her house, but I presently became a sharer in her most tender affections. I was treated by her more like a child than her servant." Again, Phillis found comfort in her religious beliefs. She was sure that Susannah Wheatley was now in heaven, in "the upper courts of the Lord."

Sadly, Susannah Wheatley died before she could see Phillis's book. In May 1774, 300 copies of *Poems on Various Subjects, Religious and Moral* finally arrived by ship from England. Phillis was able to sell all the books. By this time, she needed money very badly.

Later that year, Phillis received a letter from a wealthy Englishman named John Thornton. Phillis had met him during her visit to London. He asked Phillis if she would like to become a Christian missionary to Africa. He said that he would pay her expenses and act as her sponsor.

Phillis probably thought about the offer very carefully. Now that Susannah Wheatley was gone, she did not have enough money to live on her own. But she wrote to John Thornton, saying that she did not want to go to Africa. Phillis chose to stay independent.

Fortunately, another shipment of poetry books arrived from England. Phillis placed ads in the Boston newspapers. The ads said that the poems had been written by "Phillis Wheatley, A Negro Girl, Printed for the Benefit of the Author." Phillis was no longer labeled a slave.

Being free was just one of the big changes in Phillis's life. Susannah Wheatley was dead. Phillis's book of poetry had been printed, and many copies had been sold. At the same time, many changes were taking place in the American

THIS DAY IS PUB
Adorn'd with an elegant Engraving
[Price 3s. 4d. L. M. B
POEMS
On various subjects.——Religiou
By PHILLIS WHE
A Negro Girl.
Sold by Mess'rs COX &
At their Store in King Street
N. B. The Subscribers are reque
their Copies.

colonies. British soldiers had continued to come to Boston. By 1775, there were about 5,000 redcoats in the city. An unpopular law forced the people of Boston to board these soldiers in their homes.

Two young naval officers lived in the Wheatleys' home. The officers had once served in Africa. Hearing them talk about her native land

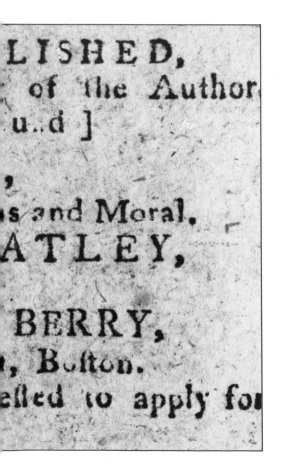

An ad in the May 1774 Boston Gazette announces that copies of Phillis Wheatley's book of poems are available to the public for purchase.

may have brought back Phillis's memories of Senegambia. In 1775, she wrote a poem called "Reply." The poem celebrates Phillis Wheatley's African roots. She praises the beauty of the land and describes its "native grace." "Reply" is the first known literary work in which an African American praises his or her heritage.

As Phillis was writing about her native land, the American colonies and Great Britain moved steadily toward war. More troops and British ships had come to New England. Colonial men had gathered all the guns and ammunition they could find. They formed groups of soldiers called *minutemen*. These men were trained to be ready at any minute to fight against the redcoats.

General Thomas Gage was in charge of the redcoats in Boston. General Gage heard that the colonists were storing their guns and other weapons in Concord, a city near Boston. He decided to send his troops to destroy these colonial arms on April 18, 1775.

Several patriots had heard that General Gage and his troops were coming. They rode on horseback to warn the minutemen about the redcoats. "The British are coming!" shouted the men on horseback. Among the patriotic horsemen was the well-known silversmith Paul Revere.

Minutemen shot at General Gage and his troops when they arrived in Lexington, a village near Concord. British troops killed eight of the Americans. The redcoats moved on to Concord and destroyed the guns and other weapons that the colonists had stored there. But as they marched back to Boston, minutemen hiding along the roadside attacked them. After this fighting ended, more British soldiers than American militiamen had been killed.

Soon thousands of Bostonians left the city. Most of them were Tories. Among them was John Wheatley, who was loyal to the British crown. Phillis sided with the patriots, but she left the city, too. She moved into the house of the Wheatleys'

daughter, Mary, in Providence, Rhode Island.
Mary's husband, John Lathrop, was a minister
there.

Phillis began to write again after she
moved to Providence. One of these poems, which

On April 19, 1775, British redcoats open fire on colonial minutemen at Lexington, Massachusetts. The fighting was the first military battle of the American War of Independence.

was 42 lines long, would soon increase her fame and lead to an important event in her life. In October 1775, Phillis sent the poem to the man whom it praised: General George Washington, leader of the American troops.

The poem called General Washington a "great chief, with virtue on thy side." Washington was, of course, very busy training and leading his soldiers. But he did finally read the poem and wrote a note to his secretary about it in February 1776. He said that the poem showed "poetical genius." It seems clear from his note that he did not know that Phillis Wheatley was already famous in several colonies for her work. He also did not know at that time that Phillis was a former slave.

General Washington wrote a letter to Phillis. He thanked her for the poem and praised her talent. He invited the young poet to visit him at his headquarters in Cambridge, Massachusetts.

That is how Phillis Wheatley came to be among the visitors who called upon General Washington one March day in 1776. She waited in her simple dress and cap, the only woman in the group of callers. The others were political leaders and men who might give the troops the money and supplies they needed to fight for independence.

Once again, Phillis had achieved something quite remarkable. Colonial women, especially blacks, were not usually involved in government business. They were scarcely expected to meet such an important military officer. Yet General Washington had invited Phillis to visit. In past years, Washington had not shown much interest in literature, but he had praised the writing of Phillis Wheatley.

The meeting was brief, and no one is sure what Phillis and the general talked about. A month later, the *Pennsylvania Gazette* featured the poem Phillis had written to honor Washington. Its stirring words may have inspired other Americans who admired Washington and wished him success in battle. The poem had also given Phillis Wheatley the rare chance to meet the man who would become the first president of the United States.

General George Washington (center) watches the British leave Boston in March 1776. When Phillis returned to Boston in December, she found the city in ruins.

4

The Final Years

Many historic events followed the meeting of Phillis Wheatley and George Washington in 1776. The American colonies declared their independence from England. The British troops that had taken possession of Boston withdrew from the city in March 1776. They left Boston in chaos.

Phillis was saddened when she went back to Boston in December of that year. Much of the city had been damaged or destroyed. The Wheatleys' house had been hit by cannon fire during battles along Boston Harbor. To get firewood, the redcoats had cut down trees and knocked down stately churches and other fine buildings. Pews and seats had been torn from the Old South Meeting House where Phillis and the Wheatley family had attended so many services.

Phillis found few friends and acquaintances in the city. Many people had moved to other towns or had sailed back to England to live. Some had died. Phillis was on her own, with barely enough money to survive. To make matters worse, the price of food, housing, and other goods was much higher than it had been before the war.

Economic conditions in the colonies grew worse as the war went on. Early in 1778, John Wheatley died. He did not leave any money or property to Phillis in his will. Sadly, Mary Wheatley Lathrop died soon after her father. Her brother, Nathaniel, lived in London, where he had married and taken charge of the family business. After the deaths of Susannah and John Wheatley and their daughter, Mary, Phillis was practically alone in the world. She had depended on the Wheatley family for friendship, guidance, and support.

Phillis had never earned money from a job other than her writing. During the war, people had little time for such artistic activities as poetry. They were struggling to provide themselves with food and other basic needs. Even experienced workers had trouble finding jobs in such trying times.

In 1778, Phillis decided to marry. She had met her future husband, John Peters, when she was a teenager. He was a free black man who had sometimes taken letters from Phillis to her friend Obour Tanner.

People who knew the couple voiced different opinions about John Peters. One of Phillis Wheatley's early biographers said that members of the Wheatley family called John "a man of talents and information." But some thought he was "disagreeable." Another writer said that John had a gentlemanly appearance and ran a grocery business in Boston. People also stated that he possessed skill in writing and speaking. Old historical records in Massachusetts show that John Peters appeared in courts of law to speak out for other black people.

After her marriage, Phillis wrote regularly to Obour Tanner. Right after the wedding, Phillis and John lived in a very comfortable home. It was located on Queen Street (today's Court Street), a fine neighborhood in Boston. Phillis did not say

Members of the Continental Congress sign the Declaration of Independence on July 4, 1776.

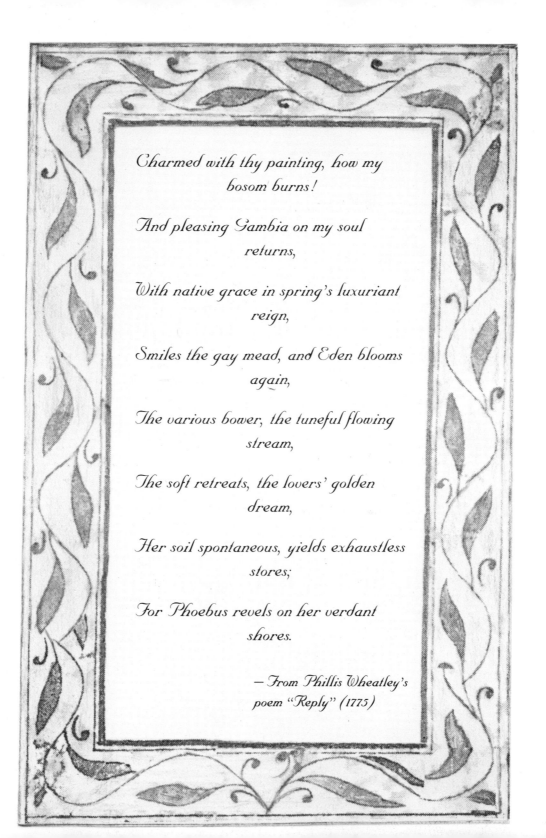

Charmed with thy painting, how my
bosom burns!

And pleasing Gambia on my soul
returns,

With native grace in spring's luxuriant
reign,

Smiles the gay mead, and Eden blooms
again,

The various bower, the tuneful flowing
stream,

The soft retreats, the lovers' golden
dream,

Her soil spontaneous, yields exhaustless
stores;

For Phoebus revels on her verdant
shores.

— From Phillis Wheatley's
poem "Reply" (1775)

much about her marriage in her letters, but they show that these married years were difficult ones for her.

Phillis still suffered from poor health. She became pregnant with her first child the year after her wedding. Phillis wrote a poem called "Sabbath, June 13, 1779" in which she asked God to give her the "strength to bring forth living and perfect" the child she was then expecting. But the baby died shortly after it was born.

Late in 1779, Phillis worked hard to find enough people to subscribe to a new book of poems. She wrote newspaper ads saying that the book would contain 33 poems and 13 letters. She planned to dedicate this second book to Benjamin Franklin. Many of Phillis's former friends no longer lived in the area. Others did not have money to buy new books. Some people remembered Phillis and her poetry from earlier years, but not enough of them offered to buy the book. She was unable to get the book printed.

Phillis was probably very disappointed that she could not publish a second book. In the early 1780s, still weak from illness, she and her husband left Boston with their second child, who had been born sometime after 1779. The family moved to the smaller rural town of Wilmington, north of Boston.

In Wilmington, Phillis's health grew even worse. She had to do more hard physical work than she had ever done before. John Peters had trouble earning a living. The home in Wilmington was smaller and far less comfortable than the home on Queen Street had been.

In 1781, the British troops surrendered to General Washington in Yorktown, Virginia. The American War of Independence was over, although the official peace treaty was not signed until 1783. Living conditions for poor people in the colonies did not get better. Phillis and John struggled to support themselves and their child. They decided to move back to Boston. Phillis went with her child to the home of Susannah Wheatley's niece. Six weeks later, John arrived, and the family moved once again.

Phillis suffered another tragedy when her second child died, in 1781. But three years later she was expecting another child. Her husband had saved enough money to start a new business, although by 1784 he had run out of money again. Massachusetts historical records state that when John could not repay his debts, he had to serve time in the county jail.

In order to pay his debts, John later sold some of Phillis's belongings. He sold some of her books, including the valuable copy of *Paradise Lost* that she had received in 1773 during her trip to London. Today the book can be found in the library at Harvard University in Cambridge, Massachusetts.

These years were very difficult ones for Phillis Wheatley. Her first two children had died, and she herself was extremely ill. The family had severe money problems. Yet she still had the spirit to write. In 1784, she published a pamphlet containing a poem that honored Samuel Cooper. Cooper was a well-known citizen of Boston who had been one of Phillis's strongest supporters for many years. When he died, Phillis wrote a mournful poem, called an *elegy*, in his memory.

In the fall of 1784, Phillis gave birth to her third and last child. She also completed her final poem, observing the end of the American War of Independence. The poem was called "Liberty and Peace." Despite her many problems, Phillis wrote a joyful, patriotic verse that starts with the words: "Lo! Freedom comes." The poem celebrated America's hard-won liberty. In the poem, Phillis also included some lines from the poem she had written for George Washington in 1776, the year the Declaration of Independence was written. The memory of that visit may have brought her happiness during these last difficult months of her life.

It is a tribute to Phillis's spirit and talent that she was able to write at all during her final

The 1834 cover of Phillis Wheatley's memoirs and poems shows a dedication to "Friends of the Africans" and includes one of her poems about native Africans.

Memoir and Poems

OF

PHILLIS WHEATLEY,

A

Native African and a Slave.

DEDICATED TO THE

FRIENDS OF THE AFRICANS.

'Some view the sable race with scornful eye—
'Their color is a diabolic dye ;
'But know, ye Christians, Negroes black as Cain
'May be refined, and join the angelic train.'

Boston.
PUBLISHED BY GEO. W. LIGHT,
Lyceum Depository, 3 Cornhill.
1834.

months. She was by then very weak, living in a home for penniless blacks. A historical record of that time calls this shelter "a common Negro boardinghouse." Phillis had no means to support herself except through whatever work she could find in the boardinghouse. Her husband was not with her and might have been in debtor's prison at the time.

Phillis Wheatley was only 31 years old when she died on December 5, 1784, after giving birth to a child. Her newborn baby lay in the bed beside her and died a few hours later. Phillis did not live to see her last poem, "Liberty and Peace," published.

Phillis Wheatley had written poems in honor of many other people. A few years before her death, in 1778, Jupiter Hammon, a slave living in Connecticut, wrote a poem to honor Phillis. He published 21 verses addressed to "Miss Phillis Wheatley, Ethiopean Poetess, in Boston, who came from Africa at eight years of age, and soon became acquainted with the Gospel of Jesus Christ." The poem ended with the words "Dear Phillis, seek for heaven's joys, where we do hope to meet."

Perhaps Phillis gained some of her strength by looking forward to "heaven's joys." She had been religious throughout her life. Her faith and her creative writing probably comforted her during those last years of loss and poverty.

A small announcement about Phillis Wheatley's death appeared in a newspaper, the *Massachusetts Independent Chronicle and Universal Advertiser*. The notice reported that Mrs. Phillis Peters (formerly Phillis Wheatley) had been "known to the world by her celebrated miscellaneous poems." It invited her friends and acquaintances to attend her funeral service at four o'clock in the afternoon on December 8, 1784.

Phillis was poor and alone when she died, just as she had been when she arrived from Africa 23 years earlier. Nobody attended the funeral service that winter afternoon. Phillis Wheatley was buried alongside her third child in an unmarked grave.

Yet the years between her arrival in America and her death had been a time of remarkable achievement. The poems of Phillis Wheatley are unique in many ways, even though they also reflect the colonial style of writing. Hers is often a brave voice, a voice calling for freedom and justice.

In order to be heard, Phillis had overcome challenges so great that they might have discouraged other, less courageous people. She faced a foreign society where she was an enslaved outsider. She quickly learned to speak a new language, English. Later, she wrote poetry in that language with more skill than most native speakers were able to. She pursued an education and a career in a society in which women and blacks were not expected to have either one. She published a book, becoming the second woman in

America to accomplish such a feat. She continued to be creative while suffering intense personal hardships.

Phillis Wheatley was not celebrated at the time of her death. But during the mid-19th century, her poetry began to be published once again. People called *abolitionists*, who worked to end, or abolish, slavery, brought her poetry to the public's attention. They made people aware of the achievements of blacks in the arts and in the fields of science and invention, among others. Phillis Wheatley played an important role in helping Americans understand that blacks have the same talents and abilities as any other people. In the face of such accomplishments, the public could not support the idea that blacks were inferior and should therefore be enslaved.

During the 20th century, Americans have become reacquainted with Phillis Wheatley's life story and her poems. She is a leading figure in the history of African Americans, in the history of

American women, and in the history of American literature.

   Phillis Wheatley has been honored in many ways over the last decade, although her grave has not been located to this day. In 1985, when Phillis Wheatley Day became an official day of honor,

On Phillis Wheatley Day, February 1, 1985, University of Massachusetts officials unveil a portrait of the poet at a special ceremony. During the celebration, the officials also named the arts and sciences building Phillis Wheatley Hall.

the University of Massachusetts renamed its arts and sciences building Phillis Wheatley Hall. An artist painted a portrait of Phillis Wheatley for the occasion. The painting is based on the engraving that appeared in Phillis's 1773 book of poetry. Massachusetts officials unveiled the portrait during a special ceremony, and today it hangs in Phillis Wheatley Hall.

But it is her work and her struggle to triumph over countless obstacles that are Phillis Wheatley's most glowing tributes. Her poetry is a lasting and inspiring reminder of the remarkable woman who was the mother of black literature in America.

Further Reading

Other Biographies of Phillis Wheatley

Borland, Kathryn Kilby, and Helen Ross Speicher. *Phillis Wheatley: Young Colonial Poet.* Indianapolis: Bobbs-Merrill, 1968.

Fuller, Miriam Morris. *Phillis Wheatley: America's First Black Poetess.* Champaign, IL: Garrard, 1971.

Robinson, William H. *Phillis Wheatley in the Black American Beginnings.* Detroit: Broadside Press, 1975.

Related Books

Adoff, Arnold, ed. *My Black Me: A Beginning Book of Black Poetry.* New York: Dutton, 1974.

Anderson, Joan. *A Williamsburg Household.* New York: Ticknor & Fields, 1988.

Dickinson, Alice. *The Boston Massacre: A Colonial Street Fight Erupts into Violence.* New York: Watts, 1968.

The Founders of America: George Washington, Thomas Paine, Benjamin Franklin, Thomas Jefferson. Morristown, NJ: Silver Burdette, 1983.

Chronology

ca. 1753–54   Phillis Wheatley is born, probably in Senegambia, West Africa.

1761   Kidnapped by slave traders, Phillis arrives in Boston, Massachusetts, and is purchased by Susannah Wheatley, wife of a wealthy merchant.

1761–70   Phillis learns English, studies literature, and begins to write poetry; she is invited into the homes of upper-class Bostonians to recite her poetry.

1771   Phillis Wheatley publishes her first major work, a poem in memory of evangelist George Whitefield.

1772   Susannah Wheatley arranges for a collection of Phillis Wheatley's poems to be published in London, England.

1773   Phillis Wheatley travels to England, where she is welcomed by her admirers; she returns to Boston when Susannah Wheatley becomes ill; *Poems on Various Subjects, Religious and Moral* is published in London; the

Wheatleys give Phillis her freedom.

1774	Phillis Wheatley writes a letter against slavery that is reprinted in newspapers throughout New England; Susannah Wheatley dies.
1775	Phillis Wheatley writes "Reply," the first known literary work in which an African American praises the culture of his or her native land; she moves to Providence, Rhode Island, as the American Revolution begins and sends George Washington a poem in his honor.
1776	Phillis Wheatley meets with George Washington at his headquarters in Cambridge, Massachusetts.
1778	John Wheatley dies; Phillis Wheatley marries John Peters, a businessman.
1779	Phillis Wheatley gives birth to the first of three children, all of whom die in infancy; she tries unsuccessfully to publish a second book of poetry.
1784	Phillis Wheatley writes her last poem, "Liberty and Peace," celebrating the end of the American Revolution.
Dec. 5, 1784	Phillis Wheatley dies penniless in a Boston boardinghouse.

Glossary

abolitionist   a person who supported the movement to abolish, or end, slavery and the slave trade in the United States

asthma   a disease of the lungs that is often caused by allergies and that is characterized by coughing and difficulty in breathing

Boston Massacre   a riot in Boston on March 5, 1770, between a group of colonists and British troops, who in self-defense killed five men

colonial America   the 13 British colonies that became the original United States of America

elegy   a poem written in memory of someone who has died

minutemen   a group of armed men pledged to join battle at a minute's notice just prior to and during the American Revolution

pamphlet   an unbound booklet, usually with a paper cover

Parliament   the British law-making body of government, made up of the House of Lords and the House of Commons

patriot during the American Revolution, a person who sided with the American colonies

plantation a large farm on which crops, such as cotton, tobacco, or sugar, are grown and harvested

preface a statement or essay introducing a book

prejudice a judgment or opinion, usually negative, that has been formed about something or someone before all the facts are known

Puritans members of a strict Protestant church who wanted to simplify the ceremonies and creeds of the Church of England and who believed in strict religious discipline

quill a writing pen made from a goose feather

Stamp Act an act passed in 1765 by the British Parliament that required people in the American colonies to buy stamps to place on all official documents and printed matter, such as newspapers and pamphlets; the money that the British collected was to be used in America for protecting and securing the colonies

Tory during the American Revolution, a person who sided with the British government

tuberculosis a contagious disease caused by a very small organism that primarily injures the lungs

Index

Victoria Sherrow is a freelance writer who, with her husband and three children, lives in Westport, Connecticut. She holds an M.S. degree in an interdisciplinary program in community mental health from Ohio State University. She has studied children's literature at the University of California, Los Angeles. Sherrow has written numerous books for children, including *Wilbur Waits* (1990), *The Gecko* (1990), and *There Goes the Ghost* (1985). Her articles have appeared in *Pennywhistle Press, The Friend, Children's Playmate,* and *Pre-School Mailbox.*

Picture Credits

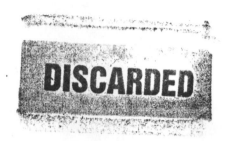